The
CHURCH
Of the
NEW TESTAMENT

Considering the Differences Between the
Apostolic and Pauline Assemblies

James Willingham

DISPENSATIONAL
PUBLISHING HOUSE, INC.

The Church of the New Testament: *Considering the Differences Between the Apostolic and the Pauline Assemblies.*

Copyright © 2018 James Willingham
Cover: Leonardo Costa
Cover and Illustrations © 2018 DispensationalPublishing House, Inc.

All rights reserved. This book or any portion thereof may not be reproduced or used in any manner whatsoever without the express written permission of the publisher except for the use of brief quotations in a book review.

Scriptures quoted as KJV are taken from the KING JAMES VERSION (KJV).

Printed in the USA
First Edition, Second Printing, 2018
ISBN: 978-1-945774-23-2

DispensationalPublishing House, Inc.
PO Box 3181, Taos, NM 87571

www.dispensationalpublishing.com

Orders by U.S. trade bookstores and wholesalers. Please contact the publisher:
Tel: (844) 321-4202

2 3 4 5 6 7 8 9 10 1

This book is dedicated to the glory of God in the hope that it helps believers in Jesus Christ better understand their role as believers and members of His church.

Soli Deo gloria

Table of Contents

Acknowledgments VII
Foreword IX

Introduction 1
What Is Meant by "Church" 3
What This Study is Not 5

Assumptions and Base Understandings 7
Jesus Died for the Sins of All 8
Literal Biblical Interpretation 8
Rightly Dividing the Word 10
The Kingdom of God Is a Physical Kingdom 13

Overview of the Two Assemblies 15
Why Does It Matter If There Are Differences? 15
Comparing the Differences 17
Why the Differences? 22

Digging Deeper 27
Membership 27
Location 34
Purpose 36
Message 40

Growth 45
Prophetic Revelation of the Assembly 47
Leadership/Elders.. 48
Giving to the Assembly 49
Jewish Law 54
Holy Ghost/Spirit 57
Fruit of the Spirit... 59
Discipline.. 62
Servants/Deacons 66
What Happened in Ephesus?.. 67

Conclusion 71

ACKNOWLEDGMENTS

Thank you to Dr. Randy White for starting me (as well as countless others) on a path of deeper biblical study and understanding several years ago and his continued dedication to the study of the Word.

Thank you to my family, especially my wife Jenna, for being my support and sounding board.

Thank you to Pastor Coleman Philley for his comments, suggestions, and critiques - all while keeping an open mind.

FOREWORD

Everyone has heard a preacher speak of "the New Testament church." We've taken this general term, without thought or inspection, and concluded that the church in the New Testament was a unified whole with a continuity that lasts to this day.

In this short book, James Willingham questions those assumptions. In doing so, I think he provides an excellent argument and a very needed service.

And it really does matter! Should the church seek to exercise the so-called sign-gifts that were very much part of the "New Testament church?" Should the church member sell possessions and live a collective lifestyle, like the "New Testament church" did? The questions and the implications are fundamental to the doctrine and practice of the church today.

James Willingham is a layman, a faithful churchman, a deacon, a loyal friend to his pastor, and a diligent student of the Word. He is also an engineer, and the precise thinking and healthy skepticism that he brings to this work will be a blessing to today's church, I'm convinced.

In dispensationalism, there is a long tradition of positive theological influence coming from laymen. Sir Robert Anderson made his career in Scotland Yard and his works have prodded dispensational investigation for over 100 years. C.I. Scofield was a lawyer before becoming a Pastor, and his legal mind built a great case for rightly dividing the Word. William Kelly was an editor who helped bring dispensational thinking to the masses. This tradition continues, I pray, in this new work by a young engineer who is digging into Scripture, asking tough questions, and coming up with logic based answers that are faithful to the rightly divided Word.

Don't expect the book to "sit well" as you begin to read it. This book is not for those who want a business-as-usual approach. Rather, it is for those who want to be honest with the clear words of Scripture, especially the book of Acts, as it relates to the church and the Christian life today.

So you hold in your hands a practical book, a frightening book, a shocking book, and—I pray—a book that is useful for your own life and doctrine.

Until He Comes!
Dr. Randy White,
Taos, NM

INTRODUCTION

An observation of the activities of the early believers in the New Testament will reveal how the church of the early book of Acts seemed to operate differently than how Paul later instructed believers to conduct themselves in the epistles. When the subject is approached with precision and intellectual integrity, one must notice that there appears to be a separate set of rules for each of these "churches," that is, for the church in early Acts as compared to the church in mid to later Acts.

There are so many differences between the two groups that it is hard to lump the characteristics of both together into one set of standards for a modern-day church without some serious twisting, allegorizing, and spiritualizing of the scriptures. So, what are the differences between each "church," and which "church" had it right? Which set of guidelines or instructions should be followed today, or does it even matter? Why is the word "church" written here in quotation marks?

These questions will be addressed by taking a deeper look into the first assembly of believers in the book of Acts and studying how their way of conducting "church" differed in distinct ways from the assembly of believers (some of whom were the same believers) later instructed by the Apostle Paul. For the purpose of this comparison, the two assemblies will be referred to as the "Apostolic" assembly and the "Pauline" assembly, respectively. The Bible describes these two sets of assemblies in great detail. A comparison of their similarities and a hard look at their differences will help bring about an understanding of not only what the believers did but also the theological underpinnings of their actions. Prayerfully, this study will lead to a better biblical understanding of what should be expected from today's church and believers in order to avoid confusion and, rather, bring glory to the Lord.

What Is Meant by "Church"

A word study is often a reasonable place to start in any biblical research. This allows for an inspection of what the Hebrew or Greek text actually says rather than coming to a conclusion based off of the reader's interpretation of the translated version of the text in question. In some cases, a word study will clarify the actual meaning of a passage and, in turn, may answer many questions from the start.

Unfortunately, this is not the case with the word "church." The word "church" in the New Testament is translated from the Greek word εκκλησία (*ekklesia*), which at its base means "to call out." It is most commonly translated as "church" in the New Testament, but the word is also used to describe a "lawful assembly" (Acts 19:39) or even a random, unorganized gathering or mob (Acts 19:32). An *ekklesia* is any assembly that has some mutual purpose, be it a religious, civic, or social. The word *ekklesia* came to an exclusive meaning of "church" during the later Christian era, and to restrict the word to a Christian (post-resurrection) context is anachronism, using a later meaning of the word in substitution of the author's meaning.

Because of the broad use of the word, it should come as no surprise that both of the believing assemblies in Acts (the early and the later) are described using the same word, *ekklesia.* The original Greek offers no easy insight to differentiate between the two assemblies in question, nor does it confirm that the early Apostolic gathering of believers is the same as the Pauline gathering of believers. Therefore, the fact that both groups are referred to as a "church" in English translations lends us no distinct help and can, in fact, lead to confusion if one were to look upon them as a single gathering. For this reason, the two "churches" that will be discussed in this study will be referred to as "assemblies" in order to help remove any preconceptions one might have about a church and how it functions.

Ultimately, additional exploration into the specifics of each of the assemblies is required in order to understand their purpose as well as their differences.

What This Study is Not

This is not a study of whether either assembly was "doing church right." Rather, this is a study of what the assemblies were doing, when they were doing it, and why they were doing it. Through an appreciation of the purpose behind the instructions and actions of these assemblies, believers can gain an understanding of the instructions meant for the modern-day church, can dissect the reasons behind some of the confusion present in churches today, and can avoid detracting from the glory of the Lord within the church.

This is also not a comprehensive study of the Kingdom of God. While the Kingdom of God is a worthwhile subject of study, it is not the intention of this study to fully explain the Kingdom of God except where the details of the Kingdom hold particular relevance to the actions of the Apostolic Assembly.

ASSUMPTIONS AND BASE UNDERSTANDINGS

A logical teaching is usually based on assumptions or on a foundation of accepted understandings. Many times, a teaching or point of view fails to gain traction because the assumptions are not accurate or not completely understood. So, before examining the issue at hand, here are some assumptions that this investigation into the scripture will be based upon.

Jesus Died for the Sins of All

The Bible is abundantly clear through passages such as John 1:29, John 3:16, and Romans 5:17-19 that Jesus' death on the cross was the propitiation for the sin of those who believe on Him, Jews and Gentiles alike. The faith and belief in Jesus' death and resurrection are foundational to salvation for both the Apostolic Assembly and the Pauline Assembly. Peter states this in his address to the Sanhedrin when he says, "…for there is none other name under heaven given among men, whereby we must be saved" (Acts 4:12). This study does not call into question the salvation of the members of each assembly, but rather aims to explore the actions and motivations of the believers once that salvation was received.

Literal Biblical Interpretation

This study will assume that God, through the Holy Spirit, has delivered the Bible to us and that the words of the text have a plain, discernable, and unalterable meaning.

At times, a study of the underlying Greek word is necessary to understand the original meaning of the author and not just the English interpretation. The original words are to be taken in their literal, historical, contextual meaning and not to be taken as an allusion or representation of something else unless obviously shown in the context to be such. Re-interpretation of the scriptures is to be avoided unless deliberately shown by the scripture itself, such as in the instance of parables or certain prophecy.

Important emphasis will be made to ensure that the audience of the text is clear. Many times in churches today, the present-day church or believer is read into the passage in order to apply the message to today's readers rather than to the original audience. A popular instance of this is seen in the replacement of Israel in the Old Testament with the church of today (Pauline Assembly) or, vice-versa, the Israelites of the Old Testament with present-day believers in Jesus Christ. Present-day believers are not automatic recipients of the direct promises from God that the Israelites received in the Old Testament. The Israelite promises were specifically for them and there are other promises for the believer today. Mixing the two promises into one application can create confusion and lead to the misinterpretation of further passages about a promise's fruition. This is not to say that the scriptures to the Israelites are not valuable, profitable, or useful, but correctly identifying the text's intended audience is essential to interpreting the scriptures and to developing an accurate doctrine for belief and living.

Rightly Dividing the Word

When there are two scriptures that, on the surface, appear to contradict each other, the Christian world today seems to immediately react by trying to make the words fit the narrative that the reader, pastor, or teacher wants them to say. Most often, one of the passages will either be ignored or an attempt to spiritualize, re-define, allegorize, or re-appropriate the words or meaning of the passage will occur. The end result of all of these actions is a twisting of the text to express something the text did not intend or an application of the words to an audience for whom they were not originally intended.

For example, believers today have a tendency to read themselves back into the Old Testament in place of the Israelites. However, the promises for the Israelites remain for the Israelites, and the fact that God is faithful to those He makes promises to should be celebrated. For example, the phrase "My people" when spoken by the Lord in the Old Testament is speaking of the Israelites, without exception. In today's Christian world, sadly, it is common practice to understand this phrase to mean all believers or the church – because, after all, believers today are His people, right? We should remember that the serpent in the Garden of Eden twisted the words of God as well. Attempting to spiritualize or redefine the scriptures is usually an awkward fit and results in theological hash mash. This can leave people confused because they do not understand when they should spiritualize the text, they are frustrated because what the Bible now "says" does not actually hold true in real life, or skeptical (rightfully so!) that there is no basis for what was essentially made-up to forcefully apply a passage to a situation where it was not intended.

When encountering these seemingly contradictory passages, it is important not to make things up beyond the scriptures, but rather dive deeper into the scriptures to find the parameters where the passage holds true and see how the scripture was intended to be applied - and to whom. In the book of Second Timothy, Paul writes, "Study to show thyself approved unto God, a workman that needeth not to be ashamed, rightly dividing the word of truth" (2 Tim. 2:15). The scriptures were not written to be a mystical cypher that only a select few should be able to interpret and understand. Paul continues, "All scripture is given by inspiration of God, and is profitable for doctrine, for reproof, for correction, for instruction in righteousness: that the man of God may be perfect, thoroughly furnished unto all good works" (2 Tim. 3:16-17). We should be as the Bereans who "searched the scriptures daily, whether those things were so" (Acts 17:11). When studied truthfully and in-depth, the pieces of scripture come together like a jig-saw puzzle and harmonize in a beautiful way that requires no extra-Biblical explanation in holding true.

The Kingdom of God Is a Physical Kingdom

Many times in Christian theology, the Kingdom of God has been spiritualized into a non-physical Kingdom that exists in the hearts of believers. However, this is definitely not how the Bible speaks of it:

- The Kingdom of God is a physical Kingdom on the earth, which is yet to be established, with Jerusalem as its capital where the Lord shall reign. (Jer. 23:5, 31:38-40; Isa. 2:2-4, 4:3-5, 24:23, 62:1-7; Joel 3:1, 16-17).

- This Kingdom will be established, first, over a regathered, restored, and converted Israel and, then, is to become universal over all the earth. (Psa. 2:6-8; Isa. 11:10-13; Jer. 30:7-11; Ezek. 20:33-44, 37:21-28; Zech. 9:10, 14:16-21).

- This Kingdom is only established after judgment over the Gentile world powers, and the Kingdom will last forever. (Psa. 2:2-4; Isa. 9:7; Dan. 2:35, 44-45, 7:26-27; Zech. 14:1-9).

Understanding the Kingdom as the time of the future, physical reign of the Messiah is a very important concept to grasp because accepting the Kingdom as a spiritual Kingdom leads down a slippery slope that eventually dissolves the distinction between believers today and the nation of Israel. The Bible spells out specific and different paths for each.

OVERVIEW OF THE TWO ASSEMBLIES

There are many distinct differences between the first assembly of believers established by the Apostles (Acts 1-8) and the assemblies of believers that were established once Saul was converted and began to share Jesus with the Gentiles (Acts 9:15).

Why Does It Matter If There Are Differences?

The Bible is the believer's sole source of authority in matters of faith and how that faith should manifest itself in the believer's life. This is especially true when it comes to how bodies of believers congregate and worship the

Lord. Therefore, it is important that a clear distinction be made between the two assemblies of believers found in the New Testament. There are clear differences as to how each assembly addressed specific aspects of a believer's faith, such as the receiving of the Holy Ghost and certain responsibilities of, and to, the assembly. If one were to try to lump both the Apostolic example and Pauline directives together, there would be contradictions between how a church should function in spiritual and physical matters.

The lack of clear distinction between these two New Testament assemblies has led to many differing denominational beliefs that mischaracterize and misapply the scriptures in churches today. Unfortunately, this has led to many situations where believers become discouraged with the church as a whole. This lack of clear distinction can also serve as a hotbed of debate amongst church members and can cause confusion and frustration to the believer (both new and old) looking for Biblical direction. The correct reaction is to dig deeper into the Word and rightly divide it.

Comparing the Differences

Following is a chart comparing the Apostolic Assembly and the Pauline Assembly on a variety of spiritual and logistical matters. Understanding the differences between these assemblies is essential in maintaining a clear understanding of what is to be expected of a church today. The scripture references listed are not exhaustive but provide a basis for comparison and examination.

Aspect	Apostolic Assembly	Scripture Reference	Pauline Assembly	Scripture Reference
Membership	Jews (and proselytes) only	Acts 2:5, 2:22, 3:12, 11:19, 18:28*	Jews and Gentiles	Acts 9:15; Gal. 3:28
Location	Jerusalem, Judea, Galilee, Samaria, Ephesus*	Acts 9:31; Acts 18:24 – 19:7*	Unto the ends of the earth	Acts 13:47
Purpose	Preparation for the Kingdom by being witnesses of Christ in Jerusalem, Judea, Samaria, and the uttermost part of the earth	Acts 1:8	Spread the word to the lost and send preachers	Rom. 10:13-15
			Prepare for spiritual warfare	Eph. 6:10-17
	Preach and testify of Christ's salvation and the coming judgment associated with His Kingdom reign which was at hand	Acts 8:12, 10:42-43; Psa. 67, 110; Isa. 9:6-7	Teaching, reproof, correction, training in righteousness	2 Tim. 3:16
			Encouragement, exhortation, and comfort of one another	1 Thes. 5:11; Heb. 10:24-25
	Prepare the nation of Israel to accept their Messiah	Acts 2:38-40, 3:19-26	Look toward the rapture	1 Thes. 4:17

Message	Believe, Repent, Be Baptized	Lk. 3:3; Jn. 3:5; Acts 2:38, 3:19, 8:12, 8:22	"…confess with thy mouth…and believe in thine heart…"	Acts 10:43; Rom. 10:9
Growth	Grew quickly	Acts 2:41, 2:47, 4:4, 5:14, 6:7, 9:31	Grew quickly	Acts 13:43, 14:1, 16:5, 17:4, 17:12, 17:34, 18:8
	Went to the people	Acts 3:1, 4:1	Went to the people	Acts 13:5, 17:18
	Members ministered and taught others individually	Acts 8:26-40	Members ministered and taught others individually	Acts 18:24-25
Prophetic Revelation of the Assembly	Prophesied of in scripture	Matt. 16:18	The age where there was no distinction between Jew/Gentile was a mystery until revealed to Paul and Peter in Acts 9 and 10	Rom. 11:25; Eph. 3:1-6; Gal. 1:12

Aspect	Apostolic Assembly	Scripture Reference	Pauline Assembly	Scripture Reference
Leaders/Elders	Apostles and Prophets	Acts 4:35, 15:2-6, 21:8-9	Local appointed elders	Acts 13:1; Titus 1:5
	Elders	Acts 15:4,6	Qualifications of elders	Titus 1:6-9; 1 Tim. 3:1-8
	Local Teachers/Preachers	Acts 8:4	Local Teachers/Preachers	Acts 18:24-25
Giving to the Assembly	Sold all and gave all, the assembly provided as each man had need	Acts 2:44-45, 4:32-35; Ezek. 36:29-30; Lk. 3:11, 18:18-25	Provide for your family	1 Tim 5:8
			Every man to give as he has purposed in his heart	2 Cor. 9:7
Jewish Law	Continued in the Law and traditions such as times of prayer/worship at the temple	Acts 1:12, 2:46, 5:12	Freedom from the Law but to be respectful of those who observe it; Do not cause a believer to stumble	Acts 15:19-20; Rom. 14:13-15; 1 Cor. 8:1-13
Holy Ghost/Spirit	Received through the laying on of hands	Acts 8:17, 9:17, 19:6*	Received immediately to those who believed	Acts 10:44, 11:15-18

	Speaking in Tongues	Yes	Acts 2:4, 10:46, 19:6*	Yes, but would fade away	1 Cor. 13:8-12
	Prophecies	Yes	Acts 2:17-18, 19:6*	Yes, but would fade away	Acts 11:28; 1 Cor. 13:8-12
	Signs/Miracles	Yes	Acts 2:43, 3:6-7, 5:12-16, 6:8, 8:6, 9:36-43	Yes, but ended within Paul's lifetime (he was unable to heal his closest friends)	1 Tim. 5:23; 2 Tim. 4:20; Philip. 2:27
Fruit of the Spirit	Love, joy, peace, longsuffering, gentleness, goodness, faith, meekness, temperance	Not all listed specifically, but alluded to in Kingdom context	Matt. 5:3-12	Yes	Gal. 5:22; Eph. 5:9
	Discipline	Swift and severe – an example of Kingdom judgment	Acts 5:1-11; Jer. 23:5	Person was to be put away from the church, but restoration is possible	1 Cor. 5:5-13; Titus 3:9-11; 2 Thes. 3:6-15; Gal. 6:1; Rom. 16:17-18
	Servants/Deacons	Yes, qualifications listed	Acts 6:1-7	Yes, qualifications listed	1 Tim. 3:8-13

* See section "What Happened in Ephesus?"

Why the Differences?

The obvious question that needs to be addressed is: why are there so many differences between the two assemblies in the first place? Why did the Apostolic Assembly conduct itself one way, when just a few chapters later in Acts, and in the remainder of the New Testament, the Pauline Assemblies are found doing something different? The short answer is that every aspect of the Apostolic Assembly was directed toward preparing for the imminent arrival of the Kingdom of God that would arrive once Israel accepted Jesus as their Messiah and King. However, a deeper analysis into that assertion should be compiled in order to illustrate the proof and to look further into how preparing for the arrival of the Kingdom of God affected the Apostolic Assembly.

The Context

An understanding of the context of the Apostolic Assembly is a good place to start when studying the reasons behind the differences between the Apostolic and Pauline assemblies. Luke's account gives much insight into the context of the assemblies because he is also the author of the book of Acts. At the end of the gospel of Luke, Jesus had been crucified, was buried for three days, and rose again. Jesus, then, continued His ministry once risen; He appeared to the two disciples walking from Emmaus and then to ten apostles (Judas being dead and Thomas not being present). During both instances, Jesus helped them to understand the prophetic nature and requirement of His death, burial, and resurrection.

The book of Acts begins with a passage that lays out some very important information, including what would be the primary concern of the Apostolic Assembly. Acts 1:3-8 states that Jesus taught the apostles for forty days - and He spoke on a directed, specific subject: the Kingdom of God. Imagine the level of insight that the apostles must have had about the Kingdom after forty days of teaching from Jesus Himself. After these forty days, the apostles asked the only question that was left to be answered – will it happen now?

Did the Jews Reject Jesus When They Crucified Him?

There is another piece of information that is easy to overlook in this passage. Look closely at the question that the apostles asked of Jesus in Acts 1:6. Who was the Kingdom for? It is often taught as an obvious reality that, since Jesus had already been rejected by Israel through the crucifixion, then the Kingdom must now be for everyone, Jew and Gentile alike. In contrast to this theological assumption, however, the apostles ask about the Kingdom that was to be restored to Israel. One could assume that the apostles failed to understand how the Kingdom would work. However, this is doubtful, as they had just spent forty days learning specifically about the Kingdom from Jesus Himself. It is important to understand that the crucifixion did not represent Israel's ultimate rejection of their Messiah. Jesus acknowledged this on the cross when He said, "Father, forgive them; for they know not what they do" (Lk. 23:34). Jesus' crucifixion was prophesied in the Old Testament and was a requirement for the propitiation of the sin of the world, whether the Jews accepted Jesus as the Messiah or not. Jesus taught this to Nicodemus (Jn. 3:14) before His death and to His disciples upon His resurrection (Lk. 24:27-28, 44-45).

There are two clues in the Acts 1:3-8 passage that point to a continuing offer of the Kingdom. One clue is that Jesus spent forty days teaching His disciples about the Kingdom. If the Kingdom offer was no longer valid, then why would He do this? He did this so that the apostles could teach the nation of Israel what it must do in order to accept the Messiah and prepare for the Kingdom. Another clue is that Jesus made mention of John the Baptist. What was John's proclamation to the people? "Repent ye: for the Kingdom of heaven is at hand" (Matt. 3:2) and "he that cometh after me is mightier than I …he shall baptize you with the Holy Ghost, and with fire" (Matt. 3:11). The time of the coming Kingdom was still upon them and the Kingdom offer for Israel was still on the table, should the nation accept it.

When Was the Kingdom Offer Set Aside?

There does not appear to be a specific point in Acts of when God retracted the offer of the Kingdom from the Jews. Instead, there appears to be a gradual transition from the age of the Kingdom offer to the "church age" that we know today. This transition appears to begin with the persecution of the believers in Acts 7-8 by the Jewish leaders and the conversion of Saul in Acts 9. Ultimately, had the Jewish nation (including the Jewish leaders) turned to Jesus as the Messiah, the Kingdom age would have begun as promised. However, this eventually became impossible once Jerusalem and the temple were destroyed in the year AD 70.

In studying prophecy, it becomes clear that the Kingdom offer will once again be made to Israel, after the rapture of the church. The book of Revelation describes what will happen in the end times when the nation of Israel will turn to their Messiah and the Kingdom of God will be established.

DIGGING DEEPER

Analyzing the similarities and differences between the two assemblies, keeping in mind that the Apostolic Assembly was preparing for the Kingdom of God, sheds a light on why they participated in certain activities and why there are differences between the two assemblies.

Membership

The Old Testament is predominately a book about God's chosen people, the Jews, through whom the Savior of the world was provided and "all the nations of the earth be blessed" (Gen. 22:18). The majority of the promises in the Bible are written to the Jews, including the promise of the coming Kingdom that will be established over all the earth. It was this physical Kingdom that Jesus taught the apostles about for forty days prior to His ascension (Acts 1:3) and that they were expecting Jesus to restore soon (Acts 1:6).

After the ascension, the apostles began to preach only to the Jews. They made it a point to preach in the temple and synagogues where Jews were, proclaiming the risen Messiah. When speaking to a crowd, they were careful to address the Jews among them (Acts 2:22) and speak of the promises that God had made to the nation of Israel. Why was this - were they prejudiced against the Gentiles? No, the apostles had a firm understanding that the Kingdom of God was to be for the Jews. There were to be some Gentile nations that would serve the Messiah (Isa. 60:3), but there were others that the Messiah would break "with a rod of iron" (Psa. 2:9). The apostles understood that the Gentiles would eventually be redeemed (Zech. 14:16), but this was to be after the Kingdom was established and judgment doled out to the nations. The next event to happen on the prophetic timeline was the establishment of the Kingdom. Therefore, the apostles were set about the task of ensuring that the Jews accepted the Messiah and were prepared for this Kingdom.

It was not until the Kingdom offer was rejected, and thus postponed, by the nation of Israel that the Lord appeared to Saul, later known as Paul, in order to reach the Gentiles. Three years after his conversion, Paul visited Peter and James in Jerusalem for fifteen days (Acts 9:26; Gal. 1:18), where it is safe to assume that Paul discussed his conversion and its meaning with them since Paul had already been preaching to the "heathen" in Arabia and Damascus (Acts 9:19; Gal. 1:16).

After Paul's visit, Peter preached about salvation to the Gentiles in Acts 10:34. Notice, before Peter's sermon to the Gentiles, how Peter was extremely confused by the vision of the sheet from the Lord (Acts 10:9-17) and the leading of the Holy Spirit that signaled the inclusion of the Gentiles. Paul had already shared his conversion and revelation with Peter, so why did Peter still not understand? Peter was confused because this was not part of the original instructions that Jesus had left with the apostles. Jesus had instructed the apostles to prepare the Jews for the Kingdom by accepting Jesus as the Messiah. However, a transition was beginning that Peter eventually had to defend to the other apostles when he returned to Jerusalem after preaching to the Gentiles. The apostles had a hard time comprehending the inclusion of the Gentiles outside of the Law, circumcision, and prophecy that had been given. Indeed, this was a mystery and a revelation to Paul and to Peter that was separate from what the Apostolic Assembly had known and had been preparing for.

What about the "Great Commission"?

Many people would point to Matthew 28:18-20, which is known as the "Great Commission," as direction from Jesus to all believers to evangelize all people throughout the world. Acts 1:8 is also often used in this manner today as Jesus gives direction to "be witnesses unto me both in Jerusalem, and in all Judaea, and in Samaria, and unto the uttermost part of the earth." Additionally, Luke 24:47 is often used to support this position as Jesus stated that "repentance and remission of sins should be preached in his *[Christ's]* name among all nations, beginning at Jerusalem."

Evangelization throughout the world is a biblical imperative (Rom. 10:14-15); however, to use Matthew 28:18-20, Acts 1:8, and Luke 24:47 as directions to believers today is a misapplication of scripture. As a deeper look at scripture will reveal, these were "Apostolic commissions" given by Jesus to the apostles in their task at hand of preparing the Jews for the coming Kingdom.

Matthew 28:20 tells the apostles to teach the nations "to observe all things whatsoever I have commanded you." With very few exceptions, Jesus' earthly ministry was directed towards the Jews and teaching the Jews about the coming Kingdom. Why at the end of this earthly ministry would Jesus refer to His previous commands if He intended the apostles to approach the Gentiles? This was not Jesus' intention and the proof is in the apostles actions in that they went only to the Jews to prepare them for the Kingdom.

The question remains: even if the apostles were only to reach the Jews, how is it that the apostles fulfilled Jesus' instruction to evangelize the Jews amongst all nations and to reach the uttermost parts of the earth? Luke 24:47 has already given us an idea of how this happened when it states that "repentance and remission of sins should be preached in his *[Christ's]* name among all nations, beginning at Jerusalem." It is easy to overlook how "beginning at Jerusalem" plays such a large role in this Jewish evangelical instruction. In Peter's sermon on the day of Pentecost, Acts 2:5 says, "And there were dwelling at Jerusalem Jews, devout men, out of every nation under heaven." This singular sermon reached every nation.

It is amazing how God works in His own timing. Before His ascension Jesus gave instructions to the disciples to go to Jerusalem and wait until the Spirit came unto them, which eventually happened ten days later on the day of Pentecost. What was the point of this? Jesus could have given the gift of the Holy Spirit upon the apostles immediately, slapped them on the back and said, "Get to work, time's a wastin'." However, a plan was in place, and God had brought Jews of every nation together in one place at one time to witness the signs and hear Peter's message of the risen Jesus and the requirements Israel must fulfill in order to receive the Messiah and the Kingdom.

The "Great Commission" was great - in that it gave instructions to the apostles in how they were to evangelize the Jews for the coming Kingdom. Is there harm in applying the Great Commission directly to the modern-day believer and church? Yes! First, it requires that believers would teach others to observe "all things, whatsoever" that Jesus commanded. However the modern-day church does NOT teach that believers should obey every one of Jesus' commands. For example, should believers start witnessing in Jerusalem or should believers "heal the sick, cleanse the lepers, raise the dead, cast out devils?" (Matt. 8:9). Furthermore, if every believer is to fulfill the Great Commission, why is baptism an ordinance that is only carried out by ordained clergy in many churches today? Why is it not taught that every believer is to baptize new converts? Care must be taken to avoid misapplying the "Great Commission," in part or in whole, as a direct command to modern-day believers.

Location

The Apostolic Assembly was centered in Jerusalem, as that was the capital of the Kingdom that was at hand. According to Acts 9:31, there were also gatherings of believers in Judea, Galilee, and Samaria. In addition to those gatherings of believers, Acts 2:5-11 tells of the Jewish audience for Peter's first sermon who were "out of every nation under heaven." The Bible does not go into detail about how or if the message proliferated from those that heard Peter's message. However, the fact that these were "devout" Jews does provide evidence that they most likely would have been involved at their local synagogue and would have told of what happened in Jerusalem that day to those in their land.

A possible example of this proliferation is found in Ephesus where Apollos taught in the synagogue. It is said that Apollos was teaching that Jesus was the Christ (Acts 18:28); however, Apollos and those that believed with him in Ephesus only knew of the baptism of John (Acts 18:25, 19:3). Therefore, it is possible that Apollos may have been a convert from one of Peter's sermons, as belief, repentance, and baptism was Peter's message, and helped spread the word to the Jews throughout the nations as was commanded to the apostles by Jesus in Acts 1:8.

On the other hand, The Pauline Assembly was, by nature, designed to be where the Gentiles were found, which is throughout the earth. Paul explains his command from the Lord in Acts 13:47 when he tells those in Antioch that he was to be "a light of the Gentiles, that thou shouldest be for salvation unto the ends of the earth." This language is similar to that in the "Apostolic commissions" found in Matthew 28:18-20, Acts 1:8, and Luke 24:47; however, each had a different audience in mind. Paul did not spend much time in Jerusalem, but rather abroad, in order to fulfill this charge from the Lord. Paul preached at and established assemblies in most of the known world, including many to which he would later write letters, which are now part of the New Testament.

Purpose

It has been established that the apostles had a clear mandate from Jesus in Acts 1:3-8 to preach to and prepare the Jews across all nations for the coming Kingdom. After teaching them for forty days about the Kingdom, Jesus' final words to the apostles before His ascension told them what to do – "be witnesses unto me both in Jerusalem, and in all Judaea, and in Samaria, and unto the uttermost part of the earth," and how they would do it – "ye shall receive power, after that the Holy Ghost is come upon you."

The apostles also prepared the nation of Israel to accept their Messiah as King. Peter twice preached to the Jews (Acts 2-3), and each time, Peter testified of Christ's salvation and how the nation of Israel could prepare to accept their Messiah. Peter was not the only one to preach about the coming Kingdom. In Acts 8:12, Philip preached in Samaria "concerning the Kingdom of God." The Kingdom was a primary concern of the Apostolic Assembly because its coming was imminent and directly related to the Jewish believers within this assembly.

The Apostolic Assembly was also to testify about the coming judgment associated with the Kingdom reign as outlined in Psalm 110. Peter sheds further light on this directive to the apostles in Acts 10:42 when he speaks about Jesus' post-resurrection instructions to the apostles: "And he [Jesus] commanded us to preach unto the people, and to testify that it is he which was ordained of God to be the Judge of quick and dead." The Kingdom was on its way and Jesus would reign "with a rod of iron" (Ps. 2).

Ultimately, there were many that accepted the teachings of the apostles and were ready to accept the Messiah as King; however, the Jewish nation as a whole – including its leaders – not only rejected the offer of the Kingdom, but went about persecuting (Acts 4) and killing (Acts 7) those who were prepared to accept the Messiah. This was a harbinger of the postponement of the Kingdom age.

Once the rejection of the Kingdom offer was apparent, a transition began to take place. This transition is seen through the remainder of the book of Acts, and, along with it, the purpose of the assembly changes. Outside of their faith and belief in the resurrection of Jesus Christ, almost every other aspect of the assembly of believers changed in some way. The Kingdom was no longer at hand, and an age of grace began where "there is neither Jew nor Greek" (Gal. 3:28). This was a "mystery" (Eph. 3:4-6) that had not been made known until revealed by revelation through the apostles Paul (Acts 9) and Peter (Acts 10). The purpose of which was to provoke the Jews to jealousy (Rom. 11:11). This new Pauline Assembly is the assembly which the modern-day church should look to in order to understand its expectations and purpose.

Both the Apostolic and Pauline assemblies had the similar focus of spreading the news of the resurrected Jesus and the need to believe upon Him for salvation. Just as the apostles were instructed by Jesus in Acts 1:8 to direct the evangelism of the Apostolic Assembly, Paul's instructions from the Lord in Acts 9:15 directed the evangelism of the Pauline Assembly. A model for evangelism is given by Paul in Romans 10:14-17, where preachers are to be sent so that people may hear.

Because the inauguration of the Kingdom of God was being postponed, Paul gave further instructions to the assembly of believers that encouraged a more sustainable existence in this world. Paul was preparing the believers for the long haul and knew that this world would take its toll on the believers, so he gave several instructions to the assembly that would help them to continue in the faith. Therefore, beyond the task of spreading the news of Christ, the purpose of the assembly included:

- *Putting on the whole armor of God* (Eph. 6:10-17): Paul knew that the believers were in for a spiritual battle before the Lord returned and gave an extremely vivid picture of how to prepare for that battle in order to stand firm in their faith through the power of the Lord.

- *Strengthening through the power of the Scripture* (2 Tim. 3:16): Paul pointed the assembly toward the foundation through which they would be able to grow stronger through, "doctrine, reproof, correction, and instruction in righteousness."

- *Providing comfort to fellow believers* (1 Thes. 5:11): Believers would become discouraged at times before the coming of the Lord. Paul instructed the believers to reinforce one another through the assembly.

- *Preparing for the rapture and the eventual return of the Lord* (1 Thes. 4:13-17): Believers will be reunited with those believers who are deceased and will be caught up with the Lord in the clouds at the rapture.

This is not an exhaustive collection of Paul's commands; however, these tasks encompass a broad spectrum of what the Pauline Assembly was instructed to do.

Message

There is an obvious change in the message between the Apostolic and Pauline Assemblies. In Peter's first two sermons, recorded in Acts 2-3, the message is that the remission of sins requires belief in the resurrected Jesus, repentance, and baptism. Standard evangelical interpretation dismisses the requirements of repentance and baptism in Peter's sermons, however the grammatical structure of the sentence clearly demands that these two actions be completed "for the forgiveness of sins." The requirement of repentance and baptism contrasts with Peter's sermon to the Gentiles where the only requirement is belief (Acts 10:43). Something apparently changed between Acts 3 and Acts 10 - the Kingdom was no longer at hand.

Believers must be careful in their definition and understanding of repentance. Repentance at its root means to have another mind, to have a change, or to reconsider. Some may argue that "repentance" is clearly implied as a requirement for salvation today because a change in thinking must happen for one to believe on Jesus. It is true that one must reconsider in order to believe on Jesus. However, to lump the change in mind for turning to belief in Jesus with the same repentance that was required of those preparing for the Kingdom is a dangerous leap. The determination of the meaning of a word by the meaning of its root is tempting (and often helpful), but it is the usage and author's intent that is the true meaning of the word. A study of the use of the word "repent" in the Greek scriptures will reveal the word's meaning as a change of behavior.

Peter's early sermons of belief, repentance, and baptism for the remission of sins should sound familiar. All four of the Gospels tell of John the Baptist's message which included repentance and baptism of water (Matt. 3:2,11; Mk. 1:4,8; Lk. 3:3,16; Jn. 1:26). Why were they to do this? John told them, "Repent ye: for the Kingdom of heaven is at hand" (Matt. 3:2).

Why was repentance and baptism such a focus of the Apostolic Assembly? The Apostolic Assembly was preparing for the Kingdom of God. How were they to enter into the Kingdom? Jesus told Nicodemus directly what one must do: "Except a man be born of water and of the Spirit, he cannot enter into the Kingdom of God" (Jn. 3:5). It required a regeneration of the spirit (belief and repentance) and of water (baptism). Note that a baptism, or immersion in water, was nothing foreign to the Israelites. A *mikvah* was a Jewish ceremonial cleansing that was required in order to be considered pure enough to enter the temple of the Lord. A baptism in order to prepare for the Kingdom of God made perfect sense to the Jews of the Apostolic Assembly.

Evangelical believers have for so long equated the Kingdom of God with personal salvation in the age of grace that they are unable to distinguish the differences between the Apostolic message and the Pauline message. They are often offended by any idea that repentance and water baptism from John the Baptist through Peter were required for entrance into the Kingdom.

Further evidence to the importance of repentance to enter into the Kingdom of God is revealed in Acts 8. Philip preached, and Simon the sorcerer believed and was baptized. However, Simon was in danger of not entering the Kingdom and needed to repent after offering money for the ability to give the Holy Ghost. Peter told Simon in Acts 8:21 that "Thou hast neither part nor lot in this matter: for thy heart is not right in the sight of God." What matter was Peter speaking of? The answer can be found in Acts 8:12, where it describes that Philip had preached on "things concerning the Kingdom of God, and the name of Jesus Christ." This was not a matter of Simon's belief; it was Simon's motivations, or his heart, that required repentance, or a change. If that change did not happen, it would remove him from being a part of the Kingdom of God. If the only repentance necessary for Simon was the same repentance that is necessary for belief (which Simon had, according to the testimony of scripture in Acts 8:13), then Simon would not have been in any danger.

Peter's later sermon to the Gentiles, which occurred after the nation of Israel's rejection of the Messiah and the conversion of Saul, includes the necessity of belief but is interestingly void of any mention of repentance and baptism as a requirement of salvation. "To him [*Jesus*] give all the prophets witness, that through his name whosoever believeth in him shall receive remission of sins" (Acts 10:43). After this message, the believing Gentiles were baptized, but notice that the baptism was not a requisite, as the Holy Ghost fell on the believers immediately upon belief.

This leads to the next burning question: is repentance a requirement for salvation today? According to the scriptures, the same repentance that was required by the Apostolic Assembly is not required for salvation in the Pauline Assembly. Paul describes the requirements of salvation in Romans 10:9, where he writes, "That if thou shalt confess with thy mouth the Lord Jesus, and shalt believe in thine heart that God hath raised him from the dead, thou shalt be saved." It is true that the belief and acceptance of Jesus as Messiah will result in "having another mind" and that following Jesus will turn a person from sinful ways, but it is important to not put the cart before the horse. According to the words of both Peter and Paul, repentance as it was understood by the Apostolic Assembly is not a requirement for salvation, only repentance so far as changing a mind toward a belief in Jesus.

Growth

In the book of Acts, the Apostolic and Pauline assemblies were both described as having rapid growth. There are many instances in the book where each assembly added a large number of believers to their body of members. Although there are more instances where the Pauline Assembly added smaller groups at certain times, it does not appear to be indicative of slower growth overall.

A characteristic that both assemblies shared in their growth is that the gospel was taken to the location where the people were that needed to hear the message. The target audience of the Apostolic Assembly was the Jews, so the message was preached in the temple and synagogues. In the age of grace, the audience of Paul's message was "to the Jew first, and also to the Greek" (Rom. 1:16), so there were instances where Paul preached in the synagogues as well as in the places where the Gentiles were known to be found, such as the Areopagus in Athens (Acts 17:19).

Another characteristic that the assemblies have in common is that members witnessed and taught on an individual basis. In the Apostolic Assembly, Philip witnessed to the Ethiopian in Gaza (Acts 8:26-40). This royal official can be inferred to be either a Jew or a proselyte, as he had been to Jerusalem to worship. Likewise, Aquila and Priscilla taught Apollos "the way of God more perfectly" in Ephesus (Acts 18:26).

These shared characteristics of taking the gospel to those who need it and witnessing and teaching on an individual basis should be the aim of churches and believers today when spreading the news of Jesus the Messiah to the lost world.

Prophetic Revelation of the Assembly

Jesus foretold of the Apostolic Assembly in Matthew 16:18 when He told Peter, "And I say also unto thee, That thou art Peter, and upon this rock I will build my church; and the gates of hell shall not prevail against it." There is much discussion and debate about what Jesus truly meant by this. Regardless, Jesus is foretelling of his future εκκλησία (*ekklesia*), or "called out," assembly. Is this specifically the Apostolic Assembly Jesus is speaking of?

It is known that the Pauline Assembly, where there was no distinction between Jew and Gentile, was a mystery and had not yet been revealed. Paul makes this clear in Ephesians 3:1-6 where he states that this mystery "was not made known unto the sons of men, as it is now revealed unto his holy apostles and prophets by the Spirit." No one knew of this mystery until it was revealed to Paul upon his conversion and to Peter in his vision in Acts 9 and 10.

Leadership/Elders

The Apostolic and Pauline Assemblies had similar leadership structures. Each of the assemblies was started by the apostles; either by one of the twelve (including Matthias), or by Paul. The local assemblies typically appointed, or had appointed unto them, elders to oversee the assembly. Even the assembly in Jerusalem, where the apostles were, had elders, as seen in Acts 15:2-6. Paul was also adamant about wanting to "ordain elders in every city" (Titus 1:5). This was such a crucial assignment that Paul gave instructions to both Timothy (1 Tim. 3:1-8) and Titus (Titus 1:6-9) about the qualifications of the elders.

Interestingly in the description of the qualifications of elders (and deacons) Paul does not extend any grace or leeway. Throughout the epistles, Paul expounds on the grace of God and how the believer is to exude that same grace to others. However when describing the qualifications of the offices of the assembly, no mention of grace is found. In fact elders and deacons alike are to be above reproach. It is obvious that Paul intended those in the roles of elders and deacons of the assembly to be held to higher standards.

In addition to the elders, there were those who prophesied and local teachers who taught and preached the Word. These were either believers who were local to the area, such as Aquila and Priscilla in Ephesus (Acts 18:26), or other believers who traveled teaching and preaching and who were scattered abroad once the persecution of the believers began (Acts 8:4), such as Phillip and his daughters in Caesarea (Acts 21:8) or even Apollos in Ephesus (Acts 18:24-25).

Each of the assemblies slightly differed in leadership structure, and although the gift of prophesy has faded away according the scriptures, these leadership structures give the present-day church a model to follow.

Giving to the Assembly

The instructions and requirements of giving to the Apostolic or Pauline assemblies is perhaps one of the greatest comparisons that can be used to illustrate the validity of the two separate assemblies.

The Apostolic Assembly held a very simple method for determining how much of their material possessions should be given, which was to sell everything and give all of the proceeds to the assembly. This is seen twice: once in Acts 2:44-45 and again in Acts 4:32-35. The believers sold all their possessions and gave the proceeds to the assembly. They kept nothing for themselves and had all things common with one another. Why would they do this? Again, this assembly was preparing for the Kingdom of God. The needs in the Kingdom of God would be taken care of by the Father, who would provide plenty for all, as prophesied in Ezekiel 36:29-30.

The instruction to have all things common with one another was not unique to the Apostolic Assembly. John the Baptist, who was also preparing the people for the Kingdom of God, gave instruction in the same manner. The people asked him what they should do to prepare, and he told them, "He that hath two coats, let him impart to him that hath none; and he that hath meat, let him do likewise" (Lk. 3:11). Jesus' ministry is also full of similar instructions. The most commonly known is the Gospels' account of the rich young ruler (Matt. 19:16-26; Mk. 10:17-25; Lk. 18:18-25). Jesus instructs the young man to sell all that he owns and give his proceeds to the poor. Jesus told the young man exactly what he must do to enter into the Kingdom of God. It was what Jesus' disciples had done (Mark 10:28) and it was what the Apostolic Assembly was doing.

The importance of giving up all material goods in order to prepare for the coming Kingdom was illuminated by Jesus when the rich young ruler went away sad and Jesus spoke these famous words: "How hardly shall they that have riches enter into the Kingdom of God! For it is easier for a camel to go through a needle's eye, than for a rich man to enter into the Kingdom of God" (Lk. 18:24-25). Further illumination is revealed by the fact that both Act 2:44-45 and Act 4:32 specifically state that the selling of possessions was universal within the assembly. If that was not clear enough, the consequence of not fulfilling this requirement is made known when Ananias and Sapphira sold their property but kept some of the money back for themselves in Acts 5:1-11. Then, they attempted to lie about their earnings and both dropped dead. Their deaths were not only a result of their lie but also because preparation for the Kingdom required that all be given.

There are modern-day movements that attempt to emulate this sort of assembly community. This is a dangerous and misguided notion. These movements fail to make the distinction that the Apostolic Assembly was preparing for an imminent arrival of the Kingdom of God. In fact, this did not go well for the Apostolic Assembly when the arrival of the Kingdom was postponed because they had sold all that they owned. Acts 11:27-30 speaks of the relief that had to be sent to the believers in Jerusalem by the hands of Barnabas and Saul. Present day believers should be wary of socialistic movements that attempt to mimic the Apostolic Assembly in this fashion.

Biblically applicable guidelines that believers can and should follow today were given by Paul to the Pauline Assemblies. In his writings, Paul gave sustainable guidelines in regards to giving that would prepare the believers for the waiting that they would have to endure.

In 2 Corinthians 9:7, Paul instructs that "[e]very man according as he purposeth in his heart, so let him give; not grudgingly, or of necessity: for God loveth a cheerful giver."

This is a significant shift in philosophy from the "give all or die" standards of the Apostolic Assembly. There is no doubt that a change has taken place. A further change is observed when Paul instructs the opposite of what the Apostolic Assembly practiced. The Apostolic Assembly took care of all believers communally, but in 1 Timothy 5, Paul limits the responsibility of the assembly to only those who do not have family to take care of them or who meet certain qualifications. He instructs that one should provide for his own house and warns that those who do not are "worse than an infidel" (1 Tim. 5:8).

The vast differences between these standards for giving require either an acceptance of a transition between the Apostolic Assembly and the Pauline Assembly (such as a postponement of the arrival of the Kingdom), or a twisting of the text to a ridiculous degree in order to fit both assemblies under the umbrella of one "New Testament church."

Jewish Law

An interesting aspect of the Apostolic Assembly is the continuation of the Jewish laws and traditions that were followed by the believers, and especially the apostles. There are several instances in Acts where the apostles and believers are recorded observing Jewish law such as traveling only "a sabbath day's journey" (Acts 1:12) or conducting business and praying in the temple at certain times (Acts 2:46, 3:1, 5:12). It may be argued that the Jews of the Apostolic Assembly were just following old habits or witnessing where they knew other Jews would be found. However, this continued observance was so steadfast that Peter went as far as arguing with the Lord about Jewish dietary restrictions when he had the vision of the great sheet in Acts 10:9-16. Even when instructed three times in the vision to eat, he still would not do it. This was more than old habits dying hard; the Apostolic Assembly was continuing to observe the Law because the Kingdom was at hand and the Law had not yet been set aside.

The next logical question is whether the Apostolic Assembly followed all of the Law including sacrifices? The Bible does not speak specifically as to whether the Apostolic Assembly continued to observe all aspects of the Law while preparing for the Kingdom. However it could be assumed that they must have obeyed all of the Law as the Law was a unified whole, not a cafeteria plan from which to pick and choose. Further, to enter the Temple they would have needed to bring sacrifices.

When the offer of the Kingdom was postponed and the offer of salvation to the Gentiles began, the apostles and Jewish believers faced a conundrum in regards to the Law. This age was a mystery that was revealed to Paul. However, Peter's vision in Acts 10 signified the end of the Law for the Jewish believers and the beginning of the age where there was neither Jew nor Greek. Still, the matter of observing the Law was so hotly debated amongst believers that Paul and Barnabas were sent to Jerusalem to inquire of the apostles in Acts 15. The apostles declared that the Gentiles had no obligation to the Law and asked only that they be respectful to those who did observe it.

Paul addressed believers in Rome and Corinth on dietary matters specifically. These matters were issues that were born from a continued observance of the Law by believers. In both instances, Paul encourages believers to not judge each other on their dietary habits, for "I know, and am persuaded by the Lord Jesus, that there is nothing unclean of itself: but to him that esteemeth any thing to be unclean, to him it is unclean"(Rom. 14:14). However, Paul does encourage believers to avoid any actions that would prove to be a stumbling block for other believers. So, while the action itself is not sinful, the effect it may have on others is sinful (1 Cor. 8:12).

The writer of Hebrews (a letter written specifically to the Jews) explains that because the Law made nothing perfect, it had been set aside; therefore, the Jews should not place their hope in the Law, but rather in Jesus (Heb. 7:18-22). Believers today may have a tendency to try to carry the yoke of the Law, or at least favorite, hand-picked laws, on their necks (or on the necks of others); but, a believer's trust is to be in Jesus, who we are called to be "Casting all of your care upon him; for he careth for you" (1 Pet. 5:7).

Holy Ghost/Spirit

The arrival of the Holy Ghost was no surprise to the apostles, as it had been prophesied in the Old Testament (Ezek. 39:29), spoken of by John the Baptist (Jn. 1:33), taught of by Jesus during His ministry (Jn. 14:16-26), and promised to come soon by Jesus before His ascension (Acts 1:5,8). However, the giving of the Holy Ghost is another difference between the Apostolic Assembly and the Pauline Assembly. With the exception of the initial receiving at Pentecost, during the time of the Apostolic Assembly, the Holy Ghost was only received through the laying on of hands in an act completely separate from the believer's faith in Jesus as the Messiah.

It is also interesting to note that although other believers in the Apostolic Assembly preached and baptized, the apostles may have been relied upon to perform the act of giving the Holy Ghost. This is seen in Acts 8:5-17 when Philip preached of Jesus and the Kingdom in Samaria and many were baptized. These believers did not receive the Holy Ghost until Peter and John arrived. However, others did give the Holy Ghost, such as Ananias who was able to lay hands on Saul in Acts 9:17, under the direction of Jesus, in order to restore Saul's sight and fill him with the Holy Ghost. (Incidentally, the manner of receiving the Holy Spirit in the Apostolic Assembly has been adopted today by those who believe in the so-called "Second-Blessing." If they fully understood the transition from the Apostolic to the Pauline Assembly, they would not make this theological error).

After Saul's conversion and Peter's vision of the sheet in Acts 9 and 10, a change occurred in the giving of the Holy Ghost. When Peter preached to the Gentiles in Acts 10:34-48, the Holy Ghost fell upon all who believed immediately upon their belief. This surprised the Jewish believers who were present, not only because those receiving the Holy Ghost were Gentiles, but because the giving of the Holy Ghost had not been done in this manner since Pentecost. Peter himself was so astonished by this that he made mention of it when he was recounting this occurrence to those in Jerusalem in Acts 11:15 where he says, "And as I began to speak, the Holy Ghost fell on them, as on us at the beginning." This was a change of the times that the current believers did not completely understand but were wise enough to trust God. Except for one notable exception in Acts 19:6 (See section "What Happened in Ephesus?"), which is forward of Peter's sermon to the Gentiles, the Holy Ghost is received upon faith in Jesus as the Christ (Gal. 3:14).

Fruit of the Spirit

An interesting comparison of the Apostolic Assembly and the Pauline Assembly is the differing attributes and abilities bestowed through the Holy Ghost to the believers.

In the Apostolic Assembly, the receiving of the Holy Ghost initiated an incredible time of wonders, which included speaking in tongues, prophesying, and performing signs and miracles. These were amazing events of which there was no questioning of their validity, even by those who would have had them stop (Acts 4:16). These signs are explained by Peter during his first sermon when he tells the people of Joel's prophecy of the last days (Joel 2:28-32; Acts 2:16-21). It is important to note that these signs would come about in the "last days." What does that mean? These were the last days spoken of in Isaiah 2:2-4, when the Kingdom of God would be established and the Lord would judge among the nations. This time was at hand, so the promised signs of the Spirit were being fulfilled as prophesied.

Along with the postponement of the Kingdom of God throughout Acts, the prophetic signs of the Kingdom also began to fade, with the exception of the church at Ephesus in Acts 19. As the age transitions from that of the coming Kingdom to the age of grace, the characteristics of the fruit of the Spirit transition as well. Paul states in 1 Corinthians 13:1-13 that although he speaks in tongues and prophesies, those gifts will fade away; but, faith, hope and love will endure.

There are also biblical clues that the miracles of healing also began to fade as Paul wrote his letters. There are examples of Paul unable to heal his closest friends in Philippians 2:27 and 2 Timothy 4:20, where he relied upon the mercy of God for healing and not a miracle. Also, in 1 Timothy 5:23, Paul spoke about physical infirmities that were being suffered. Notice that Paul did not tell them to seek one with the ability to heal through the Spirit as a solution, but rather to mix some wine for their health's sake.

There are some believers who insist that these Kingdom signs still exist and still occur today through the Spirit. These claims are dubious because the acts of speaking in tongues, prophesying, and performing miracles performed by the apostles were public and irrefutable; yet, little to no proof of a similar work exists today. These Kingdom signs are absent in the church today not because there is a lack of faith, prayer, or belief among the believers but because the current age contains different promises of the Spirit. The prophetic Kingdom signs will come again when the age of grace comes to a close and the age of the Kingdom is once again at hand. This is not to say that God cannot or will not heal an illness; however, expecting these signs to be manifested in the church today shows a lack of rightly dividing the Word as is instructed in 2 Timothy 2:15.

What are the fruits of the Spirit in the current age? Paul wrote in Galatians 5:22-23 and Ephesians 5:9 that the gifts that can be expected from the Spirit are love, joy, peace, long-suffering, gentleness, goodness, faith, meekness, temperance, and righteousness. Several of these characteristics are expressed within the context of the time of the Kingdom by Jesus in Matthew 5:3-12; however, these are not to be confused with what Paul described as the fruit of the Spirit. Notice that when Paul spoke of the fruit of the Spirit, he did not mention speaking in tongues, prophesying, or performing miracles. What Paul described is what believers today should expect from the Spirit in order to sustain the present day church throughout life and times of patiently awaiting the return of Christ.

Discipline

The approach to discipline within the assemblies of believers differs vastly between the Apostolic and Pauline Assembly. There are few examples of discipline within the Apostolic Assembly. This is most likely because "the multitude of them that believed were of one heart and of one soul: neither said any of them that ought of the things which he possessed was his own; but they had all things common" (Acts 4:32).

Ananias and Sapphira threatened that unity in Acts 5:1-11 when they sold a possession but held back a part of the proceeds and lied about it to the apostles. The punishment for this was both harsh and fatal, as they died on the spot. This passage befuddles preachers who attempt to apply this scripture to today's church. Whenever this passage is taught, a challenge is typically posed to the congregation to follow the example of that first "church" when it comes to their offerings by giving "everything" to the church. Of course, giving "everything" is usually redefined to mean increasing what is currently being given, whether that be money or time. Most often, the veiled threat of a similar fate of Ananias and Sapphira is alluded to or joked about should one not comply. This is insulting to the Word of God on a number of different levels. First, the Word has not been rightly divided and applied. This "church" was awaiting the imminent Kingdom of God and, therefore, was preparing accordingly. However, this is not true for today's church. If the misapplication of the passage is not bad enough, the reinterpretation of the meaning of "all their possessions" must occur in order to make it even reasonably applicable to believers today. This dilutes the passage and begins to build skepticism among precise thinkers, as it should. Finally, the fate of Ananias and Sapphira was no laughing matter. The Spirit of God would not suffer the disobedience of Ananias and Sapphira in preparation for arrival of the Kingdom of God.

The only other rebuke seen amongst believers in the Apostolic Assembly was that of Simon the sorcerer. Simon had believed and been baptized, but in Acts 8:18-19, Simon offers the apostles money for the ability to give the gift of the Holy Ghost to believers. This elicits a sharp rebuke from Peter who informs Simon that he has no part of the Kingdom if he does not repent of that way of thinking. Simon understood the severity of this and asked for forgiveness immediately.

Judgment in the Apostolic Assembly was swift and severe. This was a foretaste of the coming Kingdom judgment when Jesus is King and "shall reign and prosper, and shall execute judgment and justice in the earth" (Jer. 23:5).

In contrast, Paul gives less severe guidelines to believers about how to admonish a fellow believer who goes astray.

In 1 Corinthians 5, Paul instructs believers to put those who unrepentantly practice immorality away from the assembly. Paul also instructs the believers in Rome to avoid those with self-serving doctrines (Rom. 16:17-18) and commands Titus to put away any heretics (Titus 3:9-11). In addition, Paul writes to the Thessalonians to have no company with those believers who are disorderly and do not obey the Word; however, he does tell the Thessalonians not to treat the disorderly one as an enemy but to "admonish him as a brother" (1 Thes. 3:15). This signals the opportunity of the believers to guide believers who have fallen away back onto the righteous path. This is further emphasized in Galatians 6:1 where Paul writes, "If a man be overtaken in a fault, ye which are spiritual, restore such a one in the spirit of meekness; considering thyself, lest thou also be tempted." It is not only important to help restore the believer but to do so in the proper manner. Ultimately, the church in the current age of grace is instructed to extend that grace when it comes to discipline of the believers.

Servants/Deacons

A commonality between the Apostolic and Pauline Assemblies was the selection and appointment of servants, or deacons. The Apostolic Assembly chose seven men in Acts 6:1-7 who were in charge of distributing food among the widows so that the apostles could focus on prayer and the ministry of the Word. These men were prayed over, had hands laid upon them, and were sent to their task.

Paul described the qualifications of deacons in 1 Timothy 3:8-13, so it is obvious that the office of the deacon is still a valid position in the church today. Paul does not specifically call for the ordination of deacons in his letter to Timothy. However, it is possible that Paul felt the role was well enough understood and that only further instructions as to the character of a deacon were necessary; notice that he did not have to explain the role of the deacons either.

What Happened in Ephesus?

The transition between the Apostolic Assembly and the Pauline Assembly appears to have a clear starting point with the conversion of Saul and Peter's vision of the sheet in Acts 9 and 10. However, one particular instance appears to not follow this transition. Starting in Acts 10, there is an obvious and steady change from the indicators of the imminent Kingdom age into the age of grace to Jew and Gentile. This obvious change continues until Acts 19 when Paul found twelve Jewish disciples whom a man named Apollos had instructed in the way of the apostles (Acts 18:24-26). Acts 19:1-6 then throws what appears to be an anomaly of the Apostolic Assembly into a time that was well on its way to transitioning towards an age of grace. However, a deeper look into this account shows that this is less of an anomaly and more of a testimony towards the faithfulness of God to fulfill His promises.

The assembly of believers in Ephesus displayed all of the characteristics of the Apostolic Assembly. They were all Jewish (Apollos had been speaking in the synagogue, Acts

18:26, and "mightily convinced the Jews" in Acts 18:28) and they had believed and been baptized with the baptism of repentance yet had not received the Holy Ghost. Once Paul laid hands upon them to receive the Holy Ghost, they began exhibiting the same fruits of the Spirit as the Apostolic Assembly once did, such as prophesying and speaking in tongues. How is this possible in a time when these attributes of believers were to be fading away? It is simple; God keeps His promises.

Take a look at Acts 2:38-39. Peter, during his first sermon, instructed Israel to repent and be baptized for the remission of sins. He explained, "And ye shall receive the gift of the Holy Ghost. For the promise is unto you and to your children, *and to all that are afar off*, even as many as the Lord our God shall call" (emphasis added). The first believers in Ephesus were Jews who were "afar off" and had done exactly as Peter instructed and were, for all intents and purposes, part of the Apostolic Assembly. However, there was a promise to them that had not yet been fulfilled – that of receiving the Holy Ghost. God fulfilled this promise to them through Paul; and, as would be expected from believers in the Apostolic Assembly who were full of the Holy Ghost, they began to exhibit the appropriate fruit of the Spirit.

Paul comments on this occasion in his letter to the Ephesians. In the first chapter of his letter, Paul begins by addressing "the saints which are at Ephesus" (Eph. 1:1). A strong argument can be made that throughout the Bible the term "saints" refers specifically to Jewish believers in Jesus as the Messiah. Even if this argument does not hold true, a separate argument can be made that Paul's use of the pronoun of "we" throughout the first chapter indicates a union with those he is writing to that can most directly be linked to being Jewish as was Paul. Under this assumption from either argument, it appears that Ephesians 1 is written to the Jewish believers.

Paul goes on to mention the event from Acts 19 when he says to them (speaking of Christ), "In whom ye also trusted, after that ye heard the word of truth, the gospel of your salvation: in whom also after that ye believed, ye were sealed with that *holy Spirit of promise*" (Eph. 1:13; emphasis added). Paul is addressing the promise of Peter in Acts 2:29

that was delivered through Paul to the Ephesians. Even disregarding the assumption that Paul is only writing to the Jewish believers in the first chapter, the mention of the "holy Spirit of promise" connects most directly to that of Peter's sermons and to Paul's first visit to those believers in Ephesus. This is an excellent example of the importance of understanding the difference between the promises that are applicable to the believer today and those which are intended for a different people or a different age. The Word of God is wonderful, and what appeared to be an anomaly in the transition between the expectant Kingdom and the age of grace is actually a beautiful reminder that God is faithful and will deliver on that which He has promised.

CONCLUSION

There is no doubt that, upon comparison, there were two separate assemblies of believers with differing requirements for each in the book of Acts. Ultimately, the Apostolic Assembly transitioned into the Pauline Assembly as the offer of the Kingdom of God faded with the nation of Israel's rejection of Christ. However, the characteristics of the Apostolic Assembly were exactly what was to be expected just prior to the arrival of the Kingdom of God and will resurface as the time of the Kingdom draws near during the time of the tribulation. The actions and teachings of the Apostolic Assembly hold valuable insight and give tremendous examples of the believers' faith in the time of the imminent Kingdom of God.

God is not the author of confusion, but of order. So, what is the order for believers in the church today? Care should be taken to not confuse the actions of the Apostolic Assembly with the church of this age. Today, for the current age of the "mystery," present-day believers should follow the model of the Pauline Assembly. These instructions and promises are given by God to the assembly of believers who must be patient for their rapture and Christ's return. May God receive the glory from these believers and the church until that day.

Dispensational Publishing House is striving to become the go-to source for Bible-based materials from the dispensational perspective.

Our goal is to provide high-quality doctrinal and worldview resources that make dispensational theology accessible to people at all levels of understanding.

Visit our blog regularly to read informative articles from both known and new writers.

And please let us know how we can better serve you.

Dispensational Publishing House, Inc.
PO Box 3181
Taos, NM 87571

Call us toll free 844-321-4202

www.DispensationalPublishing.com

www.ingramcontent.com/pod-product-compliance
Lightning Source LLC
Chambersburg PA
CBHW052204110526
44591CB00012B/2068